D1525718

Breaking Loose

ALDEN ALL STARS

Breaking Loose

David Halecroft

PUFFIN BOOKS

PUFFIN BOOKS
Published by the Penguin Group
Viking Penguin, a division of Penguin Books USA Inc.,
375 Hudson Street, New York, New York 10014, U.S.A.
Penguin Books Ltd, 27 Wrights Lane, London W8 5TZ, England
Penguin Books Australia Ltd, Ringwood, Victoria, Australia
Penguin Books Canada Ltd, 2801 John Street, Markham, Ontario, Canada L3R 1B4
Penguin Books (N.Z.) Ltd, 182–190 Wairau Road, Auckland 10, New Zealand

Penguin Books Ltd, Registered Offices: Harmondsworth, Middlesex, England

First published in 1990 by Viking Penguin, a division of Penguin Books USA Inc.
1 3 5 7 9 10 8 6 4 2
Copyright © Daniel Weiss Associates, Inc., 1990
All rights reserved
The author also writes as "Joe M. Hudson."

LIBRARY OF CONGRESS CATALOGING IN PUBLICATION DATA
Halecroft, David
Breaking loose / by David Halecroft   p.   cm.—(Alden All Stars)
Summary: Star football player Matt Greene is pressured by his all-
pro father, which may cost the Panthers their perfect record.
ISBN 0-14-034546-9
[1. Fathers and sons—Fiction.   2. Football—Fiction.]   I. Title.
II. Series.
PZ7.H141147Br 1990   [Fic]—dc20   90-35974

Printed in the United States of America
Set in Century Schoolbook

Breaking Loose

1

"Hey, Josh," Matt Greene whispered, as he crouched down on the goal line for the season's first wind sprint. "I'm going to leave you in the dust."

"Oh, yeah?" Josh Bank answered with a little smile, squatting down beside his best friend in the three-point stance. "Since when do you think you're faster than I am?"

"Since right now," Matt answered, gazing upfield with fire in his dark brown eyes.

Josh glanced over at Matt, and saw the serious expression on his friend's face.

"Jeez," Josh whispered, elbowing Matt and smiling. "Don't take this wind sprint *too* seriously."

"But it *is* serious," Matt answered, keeping his eyes straight ahead. "We're not in sixth grade anymore."

The very first practice of Alden Junior High's seventh grade football team was under way, and the sun was blistering hot in the August sky. Seventh grade was the first year of organized football . . . and sixth grade suddenly seemed like a million years ago. Everyone knew that playing with real pads, and running real plays, was more serious than the pickup games they had been playing for years. But Josh didn't understand why Matt had to be *so* serious about it.

He glanced over at Matt with a grin, and knocked Matt off balance with a little nudge.

"Cut it out, Josh," Matt whispered angrily, as he hurried back into position. "Are you trying to make me look stupid or something?"

"I'm just having a little fun," Josh said, rolling his eyes.

"Well, this is *real* football, and *real* football isn't supposed to be a bunch of laughs," Matt whispered.

Josh Bank and Matt Greene had been best friends all through their years at Fairwood Elementary School. They did everything together—from building secret forts in the woods to playing all the new video games at the Game Place, to goofing around with the football in Matt's backyard. They had always been competitive, but it was always in the name of fun. Whenever they had a footrace, from one end of Matt's backyard to the other, it never mattered who won—because they'd always end up tackling each other and laughing their heads off.

The two friends had spent the whole summer tossing the football around and getting psyched up for their first taste of real football. And now the day had finally come.

"Okay, men," Coach Wright called out. "Rule number one. Whenever we run wind sprints, I want everyone to start from the three-point stance. Does everybody know the three-point stance?"

Most of the boys looked at the coach with blank faces.

"What's your name, son?" Coach said, pointing to Matt.

"Matt Greene, sir!" Matt called out.

"Everybody look at Matt," Coach said. "That's the perfect three-point stance. See how Matt's back is

3

parallel to the ground? See how his head is up and his eyes are straight ahead? I want everyone to look just like that."

"You're already the star," Josh whispered to Matt. "Can I have your autograph after practice?"

Josh loved to joke around but Matt wasn't laughing.

"Come on," Matt whispered. "Stop fooling around."

Even though they were best friends, Matt and Josh could hardly have been more different. Josh was thin and wiry—a perfect runner's body—with long bright red hair that curled out from under a cycling cap. And his personality was as fiery red as his hair. You could never be sure what Josh would say or do, and he was always talking and laughing. Matt was much bigger than Josh, and very muscular—the most muscular boy on the seventh grade football team. And he was much quieter than Josh, with steady, intense brown eyes.

Matt's eyes looked even more intense now than they usually did.

"Okay, men," Coach Wright called out. "Show me what you can do."

At the sound of the whistle, the entire team exploded from the goal line, sprinting as fast as they could toward the 50-yard line.

When they crossed the 20-yard line, Matt and Josh and Woody Franklin were leading the pack. By the 35-yard line, Woody had dropped back a little and Matt and Josh were running neck and neck. They were both natural sprinters, and they had done enough running that summer to be in great shape. Josh could feel his lungs start to burn a little, but he kept up his pace.

After 40 yards, Josh pulled a few steps ahead. He ended up crossing the goal line 3 whole yards in front of Matt, and 6 yards in front of Woody.

"Good run, Josh," Coach called out. "And good effort, Matt. I like to see that kind of intensity."

"Yeah, nice race, Matt," Josh said, bending over to catch his breath. "I thought for sure you were going to catch me."

"I will," Matt said, without smiling. "Just you wait."

After a short rest, Coach ordered everyone to line up again. At the whistle, the whole team rushed off downfield. The results were exactly the same: Josh first, Matt second, and Woody third.

"Wow," said Woody, slapping Josh on the back. "I thought you were just a great distance runner, not a sprinter." He turned to Matt. "The two of you are a couple of speed demons."

Matt didn't answer. He just walked away, hitting his thigh in frustration.

Woody was a good friend of Matt and Josh's. Whenever they needed a couple more guys to play pickup football, Matt always called Woody Franklin—and Woody would bring along *his* best friend, Jesse Kissler. The four boys had always gotten along really well. Woody was a tall, quiet, dark-haired boy. He was just the kind to notice Matt's strange behavior.

"What's wrong with Matt?" Woody asked Josh, as the two boys watched Matt muttering to himself. "He sure doesn't seem to have much team spirit. It's not like him."

"Beats me," Josh said, as all the boys lined up for another wind sprint. "Seems like he's taking things pretty seriously."

Matt lost the next set of wind sprints, too. When Coach Wright finally told everyone to rest and get a drink of water, Matt took his cup over to the fence and stood there by himself.

I can't believe I lost those wind sprints, Matt thought as he gulped down his water.

He glanced up into the bleachers, which were shining brightly in the late summer sun. Lifting his hands to shade his eyes, he scanned the seats. There was only one man in the whole stadium, sitting all alone at the very top corner. But Matt could tell who he was—and his heart sank.

Dad's here! Matt thought, turning away. *And I'm sure he saw me lose those sprints!*

Matt's father was not like Josh's father, or Woody's father, or any of the other fathers who lived in the town of Cranbrook. First of all, Mr. Greene was about twice as big as any other man in town. Second of all, he was about *ten* times as famous. Not only had everyone in *Cranbrook* heard of Big Bill Greene, but just about everyone in the entire *country* had heard of him, too. Football fans remembered the famous play when Big Bill caught the pitchout, and ran the ball for a 52-yard touchdown to win the Super Bowl.

Big Bill Greene had been one of the great running backs in NFL history. He had retired five years before, just after Matt's mother died of cancer. Matt could still remember when his father had brought home the Super Bowl ring. The ring was so big that it almost fit around Matt's wrist.

"I'm Big Matt Greene," Matt muttered to himself as he finished off his water. "Big Matt Greene can never lose. Big Matt Greene is number one."

"What did you say?" Josh asked, sneaking up on Matt from behind.

"Nothing," Matt answered, surprised. "Just talking to myself."

"This practice is tough, isn't it?" Josh said, wiping the sweat from his brow. "I'm about to melt."

"Football is a tough game," Matt answered. "If you want to play football, you have to suffer. No pain, no gain."

"I've had enough pain for today," Josh said. "Those wind sprints really took it out of me."

The wind sprints! Matt could just imagine the lecture he'd get when he went home after practice. His dad would tell him how to run faster, how to keep his head down and pump his legs. His dad would tell him to practice and practice, until he got it right.

"Coach Wright?" Matt called out, all of a sudden. "I have a request to make, sir."

"What's that, Matt?" Coach answered.

"I'd like to run another set of wind sprints."

The whole Panther squad looked at Matt like he was crazy. Even Coach Wright couldn't believe his ears.

"That's very nice, Matt," Coach said. "But may I ask you *why* you want to run more wind sprints?"

"Because I think I can do better, sir," Matt said.

He was the only guy on the team to call Coach Wright "sir"—but his father had told him to.

"I admire your intensity, Matt," Coach Wright said. "But don't you need a break? Wouldn't you like to do some blocking exercises, instead?"

Matt glanced up into the bleachers and saw the outline of his father against the bright blue sky. "No pain, no gain," Matt said.

This was Coach Wright's first year in Cranbrook. He was replacing Coach Kramden, who had taken a year's leave, and he didn't know that Matt's father was Big Bill Greene. Even though he drilled the boys hard, Coach seemed to have a good sense of humor, and everyone already liked him. He shook his head and smiled at Matt.

"You asked for it," Coach said. "Everybody line up for the Matt Greene Memorial Wind Sprint."

The team gave Matt a cold stare as they dragged themselves to the goal line. Matt knew that he wasn't making himself any more popular with his friends by calling for extra wind sprints. But he couldn't stand to let his dad see him lose.

I have to win, I have to win, Matt thought as he squatted into the three-point stance. *I'm Big Matt Greene, and I have to win.*

Matt's heart was beating like crazy when Coach

9

blew the whistle. He took off sprinting, but Josh pulled out in front of him. After 40 yards, Josh was still two steps ahead. Matt was going to lose again— in front of his father—if he didn't do something. So he put on his afterburner and somehow sped ahead of Josh, crossing the goal line one step ahead of his best friend.

Matt could feel his father's proud gaze as he lifted his arms in victory.

"Yes!" he called out, catching his breath. "I won!"

"Take it easy, Matt," Josh said. "You act like you just won the Super Bowl."

What does Josh know about the Super Bowl? Matt asked himself, as the team walked toward the blocking dummies for blocking practice. *In fact, what does he know about football? The only thing he knows about is fooling around.*

Coach Wright picked up the biggest blocking dummy, which looked like a punching bag from a boxer's gym, and held the bag in front of him.

"Matt, let's see your stuff," Coach called out. "Grab the dummy like you're going to make the game-saving tackle. Keep your head up. Hit it hard with your chest and drive through with your legs. Ready! Hut, hut!"

Matt could feel his father's eyes upon him as he

ran toward the dummy. He could almost hear his father's voice telling him how to slam into the dummy with all his strength, and dig into the dirt with his cleats. Matt hit the dummy and Coach Wright absorbed the shock.

"Nice work, Matt," Coach said. "I can see you've had some good coaching."

But Matt felt that he should have done better, no matter what Coach said. He glanced up again and saw the big outline of his father, in the far corner of the bleachers. He should have hit the dummy hard enough to knock Coach Wright onto the ground. *Then* his father would have been proud.

When Coach finally called the practice, Josh and Woody started off toward the lockers, but Matt didn't move.

"I'm about to melt," Josh said. "Let's all head over to Dairy Delight and get some sodas."

"I hear there's a new video game at the Game Place," Woody added. "Jesse told me all about it. It's called Ultra Man, and the idea is to kill as many droids as you can with these huge guns. . . . Hey, Matt, aren't you coming?"

"I don't think so," Matt said.

"Why not?" Josh asked.

"That stuff's for little boys," Matt answered.

"What do you mean by that?" Josh responded. "You hang out at the Game Place as much as I do."

"Not anymore," Matt answered. "If you want to play football, then you have to eat, sleep, and breathe football. You guys can go play video games and drink sodas, but I'm going to work on my wind sprints."

"Whatever, Matt," Josh said, as he turned and walked away with Woody.

Matt watched his friends walk toward the locker room. He couldn't believe how immature they were acting. To be a great football player meant having to make sacrifices. It meant football had to be your life. Couldn't they understand that?

Matt glanced up to the bleachers and noticed that his father had already left. The seats were completely empty, and shining golden in the setting sun. But somehow, Matt could still feel his father's eyes upon him as he practiced his wind sprints, up and down the field.

2

"I can't believe that *I* am going to be quarterback!" Jesse Kissler exclaimed in the locker room after practice, a week later. "Somebody better teach me how to throw a football . . . and soon!"

Coach Wright had just announced everyone's position. Matt had gotten exactly the position he wanted—running back, just like his father. Josh was going to be a wide receiver, which was perfect for a small, fast guy . . . "with lightning-quick reflexes," as Josh always added. Woody was going to be a defensive back, where he could do the thing he loved to do best—tackle. Dan Caner, Dave McShea, Bruce Judge, and "Duke" Duquette were all big guys, but not too fast, so they would be the Panthers' linemen.

There were no huge surprises—except for the fact that Jesse Kissler was going to be quarterback.

"I can't believe it either, Jesse," Josh said as he tied his sneakers and picked up his gym bag. "No offense or anything, but you're not exactly a speed demon."

Jesse was tall and a little goofy-looking, with a blond crew cut and a funny, flat-footed way of running. Still, Jesse was one of the best pitchers in the whole Little League baseball conference, and Coach Wright was hoping to make use of his natural throwing abilities.

"It doesn't matter how fast a quarterback is, as long as he can throw the football," Woody commented.

"Anyone who's ever faced Jesse in Little League knows that he can pitch a baseball," Josh said. "But a football . . . that's a different matter."

A football sure is a different matter, Matt thought as he listened to his friends' conversation. He was sitting away from them, tying his shoes. Since Matt was the running back, he would have to depend on Jesse's ball-handling skills on every play. If Jesse made a mistake with the timing of a handoff, or made a bad pass when Matt went out for a screen, then it was *Matt* who would look bad. And looking bad—in front of his dad—was the one thing in the world that Matt didn't want.

"Hey, Jesse," Matt said, standing up. "Why don't we go outside and work on your passing?"

"No way, Matt," Jesse said, laughing and shaking his head. "*You* may be the type of guy who stays after every practice. But *I'm* the type of guy who can't wait for practice to end, so I can go get a soda and relax."

"I think the word 'relax' has dropped out of Matt Greene's vocabulary," Josh said. "All Matt can think about these days is football, football, football."

"Listen, guys," Matt began, putting his hands on his hips. "If Jesse doesn't learn how to handle a football, then who do you think is going to look bad? *Me.*"

"Is that the only thing that matters to you?" Josh asked, shrugging. "I mean, don't you like going to the Game Place and having a soda with your friends anymore?"

"All soda does is rot your teeth," Matt answered

matter-of-factly. "We're in training. If you want a drink, you should drink milk."

"Sounds like *you're* in training to be a big fat jerk," Josh said, winking.

Everyone laughed except Matt, who could feel his face turning hot. "Okay, guys," Matt said. "If you come out and work on Jesse's passing with me, we can all go over to my dad's new restaurant and get a free soda. Deal?"

"I hear your dad's new restaurant is the best," Josh said, his face brightening. "I say it's a deal!"

"Deal!" Woody and Jesse agreed.

The four friends ran out onto the field, and Matt pulled a football from his gym bag.

"Make a circle with your thumb and finger, Jesse," Matt began, suddenly sounding like a teacher. He put the ball in Jesse's hand. "Don't grip it too tight. Keep your arm relaxed. Now, lay your other three fingers on the side of the ball. They make it spiral when you throw. And just use your natural throwing motion. You got me so far?"

"I think so," Jesse said.

"Good. I'll go out for a screen pass," Matt said. "Woody, you cover me."

Matt sprinted out ahead of Woody and turned his head to receive the pass. But Jesse's pass wobbled end over end, like a wounded duck, and fell right into Woody's arms. Everybody laughed . . . everyone except Matt.

"Now, come on, Jesse," Matt said, walking back toward the quarterback. "We've got to practice till we get it right. Try relaxing your arm. And follow through like you were pitching a baseball."

Matt kept his friends practicing for almost an entire hour, but by the end, Jesse had improved. He was throwing beautiful spiral passes.

"*Now* do we get to go to your dad's new restaurant?" Jesse asked.

"You bet," Matt answered, heading off the field. "And if you guys listen hard and concentrate, maybe my dad will teach you something about football."

Josh rolled his eyes behind his friend's back.

"Hey, Woody," Josh whispered. "All that guy thinks about these days is football. Isn't he ever going to take a break, and just be *Matt?*"

"I don't know," Woody whispered. "But I have a hunch I know what this is all about."

Big Bill's Goalpost was in the middle of downtown Cranbrook, near Danahy's Park. The new restaurant had only opened a month before, so none of the boys—except Matt—had ever been inside.

Josh, Woody, and Jesse were amazed when they walked through the door. The restaurant decor had a complete football theme: the floor was made of AstroTurf, all the waiters and waitresses were dressed like referees, and every inch of wall was covered with pictures of old football teams and posters of Big Bill Greene. On the front wall, behind the salad bar, was a huge wall-sized photograph of Big Bill making his famous 52-yard run to win the Super Bowl. And to top if off, there were 10 wide-screen TVs playing video clips from NFL history.

"What a great place!" Josh exclaimed to Matt. "You're lucky to be able to hang out here whenever you want to."

"I guess so," Matt said, shrugging.

He had never really thought about it before. Of course, he was proud of his father, but sometimes he just wanted to get away from all that old NFL footage.

Just then Big Bill Greene walked up to the boys. "Well, hello there," he greeted them.

"Hi, Dad," Matt answered. "We just came over to say hello."

"And have a soda," Josh added.

"A soda?" Mr. Greene said, shaking his head. "Aren't you men in training? Players in training should drink milk, not Coke. Now, you men go take a seat. I have a little surprise for you."

The four friends sat down in a booth, looking at all the old football rosters, and photos of teams. A second later, Big Bill came back carrying three professional-sized footballs, with his autograph written on them.

"I want each of you men to have one of these footballs," Mr. Greene said.

"Wow!" all the boys said at once. "Thanks, Mr. Greene!"

"But let me tell you *why* I'm giving these balls to you," Mr. Greene said, crossing his huge arms. "These balls are to remind you that football is a serious game," he continued. "Now, I've been to some of your practices. I've seen how you guys joke around and laugh, and talk about video games. That's fine for sixth grade. But sixth grade is over and it's time to get serious. If you want to be a great player, you've got to work. Do you understand?"

All of the boys gulped, and nodded their heads.

"Every time you men see these footballs, I want you to remember that football takes everything you've got," Mr. Greene went on, frowning. "You've got to be the best. You've got to eat, sleep, and breathe football. You've got to practice and practice,

19

and work and work. And that means practicing *after* practice is over. Does everybody understand?"

Everyone nodded, as a waiter stopped at their table and handed them four huge glasses of milk.

"Now drink that down, and don't let me hear anything more about Coca-Cola," Mr. Greene said. "Milk builds muscles. Soda is full of sugar. Remember, men, you're in training."

When Mr. Greene left, the four friends sat in silence—without so much as touching their milks.

"I guess I'm not so thirsty after all," Josh said.

"Me, neither," Woody said with a shrug.

"Tell your dad thanks for the footballs, Matt," Josh added, getting up from the table. "I told Duke and Bruce that I'd meet them at the Game Place."

"I'll go with you," Woody and Jesse said together. Suddenly, it seemed that everyone couldn't wait to get out of Big Bill's Goalpost.

"If you guys want to waste your time with video games, go ahead," Matt said. "I'll stay here and learn about football."

"Okay, Matt," Josh answered, rolling his eyes as the boys hurried out with their autographed footballs. "Have a *great* time."

Matt watched his friends leave the restaurant. When the door closed behind them, Matt sighed and looked up at the video screen, where Big Bill Greene was faking out a defenseman, and scoring another game-winning touchdown. Matt wondered if he would *ever* be good enough to please his father. One thing was for sure—he would *never* be good enough if he wasted his time playing video games.

"What's wrong, Matt?" Big Bill asked, walking up to the table. "Your friends didn't even touch their milks."

"They went to play video games," Matt said, looking down.

"Video games? Let me tell you something, Matt," Mr. Greene said, sitting down beside his son. "Those guys are a little goofy. Josh especially. If you let him, Josh will take your mind off football, and you'll end up making a mistake in a big game."

"Yes, sir," Matt said.

"By the way," Mr. Greene continued. "Coach announced the positions today, didn't he?"

Suddenly a big smile came across Matt's face.

"He sure did," Matt said proudly. "And guess what? I'm going to be the running back!"

"Like father, like son," Mr. Greene said, slapping Matt on the back and smiling. "But never forget, Matt—running back is one of the hardest positions on the team. I worked years and years to be the best.

21

When I was your age, I spent a lot of time reading about football, and working on agility drills in the backyard."

"Yes, sir," Matt said. Suddenly he didn't feel so excited about being the running back after all.

"And now that you're going to be a running back, let me give you your first lesson," Mr. Greene said, pointing up to a video screen that was showing another one of his famous runs.

"Do you see what I'm doing there?" Mr. Greene began. "The call was for a straight run, right up the middle. But when the play developed, I saw a hole opening left and I faked out the lineman. Do you see how I tuck the ball in my arm, Matt? Since you'll be a running back, always remember to keep the ball tucked in close to your body. You can bet those defensemen are going to try everything they can to strip that ball away."

Matt drank his milk and listened. He knew that once his dad got going, he would be giving him a lesson for another twenty minutes. Matt thought of his friends, having a good time down at the Game Place. That new game, Ultra Man, sounded pretty good. For a split second, Matt really wished he could be with Josh and Woody and Jesse, drinking sodas and telling jokes and zapping video droids—just like old times.

"Are you listening to me, Matt?" Mr. Greene asked.

"Yes, sir!" Matt said, snapping to attention.

j 4 a l 4 l

3

"You knew Coach Wright in college?" Matt asked his father a week later, as they walked together toward the football field. "And you haven't even said *hello* to him yet?"

"That's right, Matt," Big Bill Greene said. "I wanted to wait until after the positions were announced. If I had said hello to Coach Wright earlier, then he would have given you little advantages. And if there's one thing that can ruin a good football player, it's getting breaks from the coach. A good football player fights and works and suffers for everything he gets."

"Yes, sir," Matt answered. He had just finished his first day of classes at Alden Junior High, and now it was time for the first real scrimmage, with full gear. Matt was so scared of making a mistake in front of his father that he was actually cold, even though the hot September sun was beating down. He just *had* to show his father how good he was!

"Why, if it isn't Big Bill Greene," Coach Wright said, with a big smile. Coach walked over and shook Big Bill's hand. "It's been quite a few years." He looked at Matt and back at Big Bill. "Is Matt your son?"

"He sure is," Big Bill answered.

"Well, you have a lot to be proud of," Coach Wright said. "Matt is a very talented running back."

"A lot of kids have talent," Big Bill answered. "But it takes hard work to turn talent into touchdowns."

"Okay, Panthers, gather around," Coach Wright called out. "I want you to meet someone special."

The whole team gathered around Big Bill Greene and Matt.

"Panthers," Coach began, "This—as most of you know—is Big Bill Greene. Bill and I were on the same team in college. I saw how Bill practiced and

25

worked and made himself into one of the great running backs in NFL history. I want him to be an example to all of you."

Matt's hands shook as he listened to Coach—but they were shaking even worse by the time he got out on the field. He could feel his father's eyes on him at every moment. What if he made a mistake? What if he didn't make amazing touchdowns and spectacular catches?

Josh knew his best friend well enough to tell that Matt was nervous. So when they got into the first huddle, Josh gave Matt a friendly slap on the shoulder pads.

"Hey, Matt," Josh whispered. "Just relax. You're going to do just fine."

"Be quiet," Matt snapped. "I'm trying to concentrate on the game."

"Okay, okay," Josh said, his face turning as red as his bright red hair. "See if I try to be nice again."

Jesse called the first play. It was going to be a handoff to Matt, on three, with Josh running in from the wide receiver position to block.

Matt had never been so nervous in his life—and it was only a scrimmage! He listened to Jesse call out the count.

"Hut! Hut! Hut!"

The Panthers went into action. Matt pushed forward and snatched the ball from Jesse's hand. But where was Josh to do the blocking? All that Matt could see in front of him were the big blue and gold jerseys of the defensemen. Suddenly Matt stopped cold. It was as if his legs had turned to ice! He couldn't move an inch! A second later, Woody came barrelling in and tackled Matt for a three-yard loss.

His first real run in a real game, and Matt had completely frozen! Not only had he looked like a fool, but he had lost three yards!

"Where were you, Josh?" Matt asked angrily, as they walked back toward the huddle. "You were supposed to block for me on that play. Didn't you remember? Or were you thinking about playing video games, while I was over here getting creamed?"

"Hey, I'm sorry, bigshot," Josh said, offended. "I'm not perfect, like you."

"Quit it, you guys. That's enough yelling," Jesse said. "We're supposed to be a *team*, remember?"

Coach Wright called a time-out, and the Panther offense ran to the sideline.

"Okay, men, shake it off," Coach said. "Matt, you look a little nervous out there. Just relax and do your best. Next play is a delay left, thirty-eight halfback option. On two."

As they were running out to the field, Big Bill Greene called Matt over to the sideline. Matt couldn't look his father in the eye.

"What happened out there, son?" Big Bill asked. "It looked like you just gave up, like you didn't even want to try. You've got to do better than that. Now get back out there—and this time, play like you *mean* it."

Matt felt cold chills as he joined the team in the huddle.

"Everybody got the play?" Jesse whispered. "Thirty-eight, halfback option on two. Break!"

The Panthers had worked on this play a lot during summer practice. On the halfback option, Jesse would toss the ball back to Matt. Then Matt had the option either to run with the ball, or to pass it forward to Josh, who was delaying on the line of scrimmage before he ran his pattern across the middle of the field.

Matt just prayed that his legs wouldn't freeze up again. But his hands were shaking and he felt more scared than ever.

I'm Big Matt Greene, he said to himself, as he squatted down in the three-point stance. *I'm Big Matt Greene and I have to be the best.*

"Hut! Hut!"

Jesse pitched the ball back to Matt, and Matt ran left, looking for a hole. But nothing much was opening up, because Woody, John DeLuca, Percy Walker, and the rest of the Panther defense were reading the play like a book.

Suddenly Josh got open in the middle of the field. He was running along waving his hand so Matt would pass to him. It would have been an easy pass, and at least a 12-yard gain—maybe more. But Matt had to prove himself, so he forgot about the pass and turned toward the line of scrimmage. A second later he ran headfirst into John DeLuca, a huge Panther defenseman. When they hit, the ball was knocked out of Matt's hands and Woody picked up the fumble. Matt stood in disbelief, as he watched Woody run the fumble for a touchdown.

"I was wide open, Matt," Josh said, as the offense walked slowly toward the sidelines. "You should have given me the pass."

"It's called a halfback *option,* for your information," Matt said angrily. "That means I can do whatever I want."

"Like fumble?" Josh said.

Matt knew that Josh was right. He should have passed. And now he had made himself look even more foolish in front of his dad.

29

"Hey, Matt, what were you doing out there?" Big Bill yelled.

Matt suddenly wished he could be anywhere else in the world besides on that football field.

"Haven't you been listening to anything I've said?" Big Bill said. "First of all, you should have passed the ball to Josh. Second of all, if you're going to run, at least tuck the ball safely against your body. If you don't, you're going to be fumbling for the rest of your life. Are you listening to me?"

Coach Wright couldn't help but listen to what Big Bill Greene was telling Matt. Big Bill was yelling so loud that Coach could hear every word—and he didn't like what he heard at all. What twelve-year-old boy in the world could be expected to play his best, under so much pressure?

The rest of the scrimmage went badly for Matt, too. He *did* make a few short gains, and he *did* catch a screen pass, but for the most part, he either lost yardage or fumbled. And after every mistake, his father called Matt to the sidelines.

Coach wondered if Big Bill thought he was actually *helping* Matt by putting so much pressure on him. It seemed like Matt just played *worse* after talking to his dad. Coach knew that Matt was a talented running back, and it was terrible to watch him playing so badly. Not to mention what Matt's bad attitude was doing to the team's spirit.

After the scrimmage, Matt left with his father, while Josh and Woody and Jesse stayed behind to talk on the bench. Coach Wright was close enough to hear the boys' conversation.

"Matt blames everybody else for his mistakes."

"No kidding," Woody answered. "He thinks he's the greatest, but he isn't even playing very good."

Not only was Matt getting pressure from his dad, but he was losing his best friends, too.

4

Matt was miserable. The week after the scrimmage, he worked on his running skills every day,
and spent the evening hours in Big Bill's Goalpost,
studying the old videos. Whenever his friends asked
him to go to the Game Place, Matt always said he
was too busy. But deep down, Matt really *missed* his
friends. He was getting awfully tired of living, eat-
ing, and breathing football.

Matt thought that if he could score a touchdown
on Saturday, in the first game against North Colby,

everything would be perfect again. If he could only be the star of the game, and make an amazing 52-yard breakaway touchdown, then his dad would be proud.

But Matt wondered if he could *ever* be good enough to make his father happy.

"I want to see some hustle out of you today, Matt," Mr. Greene said that Saturday, on the way to the Alden Junior High field. "This is your first *real* game as a *real* football player. Make sure to keep the ball tucked close to your body, and cover the butt end of the football with your palm. And remember, I'm going to videotape the game."

"Yes, sir," Matt said.

It was a beautiful blue morning, with the first hint of fall in the air—in short, it was perfect football weather. But Matt didn't notice the blue sky, or the maple leaves that were already turning red along the streets of Cranbrook. He was too busy trying to remember all of the things his father had told him to do: keep the ball tucked in close, always fake the man, keep the hips up on the three-point stance, keep the eyes straight ahead.

I know I'm going to screw up, I just know it, Matt thought. *But I can't mess up! I've got to show Dad that I can be the best, too.*

33

As the team warmed up, the parents and friends in the bleachers could tell that the Panthers had all the makings of a good football squad. Coach Wright had done a great job getting the boys in shape, and teaching them the fundamentals: blocking, tackling, running, catching. Josh had become an excellent wide receiver, with his lightning speed and his good hands. Woody was a big, mean safety—but fast enough to get to the action. And Jesse had developed into a fine quarterback.

But Matt was the one whom everyone had their eye on—not only because he was Big Bill's son, but because he was such a natural athlete. Matt moved like a champion.

In the first quarter, Matt lived up to everyone's expectations. The first call of the season was for a handoff to Matt. Matt crouched down in the three-point stance, staring forward at Jesse's back. He heard Jesse call out the numbers, and on three the Panthers burst into action. Matt lunged forward and saw Jesse fade back and turn sideways. He opened up his arms and felt Jesse stuff the ball firmly into his stomach—just like he had a hundred times at practice. Then Matt saw a hole open up on the right side of the defense, and cut sharply toward it as he crossed the line of scrimmage.

A North Colby defensive back was rushing in to plug the hole, but Dave McShea, the Panther lineman, threw a block just in time to stop him. Matt tucked the ball in close to his body and jumped over the tackled players as if they were hurdles on a track. When he landed, he turned on the speed and rushed up the right sideline. After sprinting another eight yards, he was pushed out of bounds by the North Colby safety at the Alden 34, for a gain of 14 yards.

The Alden fans leapt to their feet and cheered for Matt. It was a great sign that his first play of the season had gone so well, and Matt clapped his hands as he ran back to the huddle.

"Great run, Matt," Josh said, slapping his friend on the shoulder pads as they bent into the huddle.

"Thirty-eight, pitchout left, on two. Break!" Jesse said.

38 was Matt's number, and Matt crouched down with his heart beating like crazy, imagining how he'd catch the pitchout, and then break away for an incredible 66-yard touchdown.

"Hut! Hut!"

Matt surged forward and to the left, while Jesse spun around and pitched the ball. Matt could tell right away that the pitchout was a little too high, and he felt his heart skip a beat. Would it sail over his head? He jumped as high as he could and just barely tipped the ball—enough to knock it up into the air. When he landed, he spun around and the ball fell into his hands. He could hardly believe how lucky he was as he took off running toward the line of scrimmage.

By that time, the strong North Colby defense had broken through the Alden offensive line, and two defensemen were charging toward him. Matt gave the first defenseman a nice head fake and cut around him to the left. But the second defenseman read Matt's fake like a book, and tackled him at the line of scrimmage.

Still, the crowd gave Matt a big cheer for having saved a big loss—or even a possible North Colby recovery.

The next call was for a pass, and Matt's job was to protect the quarterback. He missed his block, but it didn't matter since Jesse got the ball off in time. The pass was meant for Chuck McPhee—and it hit him right on his numbers. But Chuck couldn't get a handle on it, and the ball fell to the ground incomplete.

It was now third and ten, from Alden's own 34-yard line.

"Okay, guys," Jesse said in the huddle. "Coach just wants a first down. Thirty-eight, screen pass right, on three."

First down? Matt thought as he crouched in the backfield. *I'm going to catch that screen and run all the way for a touchdown.*

"Hut! Hut! Hut!"

Matt rushed to right, crossed the line of scrimmage and turned to receive the pass. The pass was picture perfect: just as Matt turned around he saw the ball flying toward his numbers. He caught the ball and took off running.

Ahead of him was a wall of North Colby jerseys.

I can still score, Matt thought as he cut left. But when he saw the defense closing in, he stopped short, cut back over the line of scrimmage, and changed directions. He knew it was a dangerous move, but it was the only way he had a chance of breaking free.

The defense wasn't fooled, and Matt began to get nervous as he scrambled through his own backfield. He realized that if he didn't get over the line of scrimmage soon, he would be tackled for a loss. So Matt turned forward and plunged into a wall of North Colby defensemen, for a gain of two yards.

I can't believe I only gained two yards, Matt

thought as he crawled out from under three North Colby players. *I hope Coach decides to go for the first down! Then I can really make a great play.*

But it was fourth and eight, and Coach decided to punt.

Although everyone thought that Matt had played a great first quarter, Matt wasn't all that happy. He knew he had to make a huge breakaway run, and score at least one touchdown, before he—and his father—would be satisfied.

But it was Josh who scored the first touchdown of the season. It came in the middle of the second quarter, on a beautiful bomb pass from Jesse. Josh dove, caught the ball in his fingertips, and landed in the end zone. The whole Alden cheering section went crazy, and Josh spiked the ball and did his victory dance.

Matt didn't cheer along with his teammates. *He* had wanted to score the season's first touchdown. He had wanted his father to videotape *him* spiking the ball, and doing a victory dance.

Josh came up to Matt while the offense was on the sidelines.

"Aren't you even going to congratulate me?" Josh asked. "In case you didn't happen to notice, I *did* just score our first touchdown of the season."

"Congratulations," Matt said, without looking at Josh.

"Is that all you're gonna say?" Josh asked. "I'm your best friend, and all I get is one lousy 'congratulations?' What's gotten into you? You're acting like a totally different person since football started."

"I don't want to talk about it," Matt answered. "I'm trying to concentrate on the game."

"Yeah? Well, maybe you'd better concentrate on being Matt again," Josh said, turning to walk away.

In the locker room at halftime, Matt was still angry that he hadn't scored the first touchdown—so angry that he barely listened to Coach's pep talk.

One thing's for sure, Matt thought, as the team ran back onto the field. *I'm going to score a touchdown this half.*

When the second half started, the scoreboard read Alden 7, North Colby 0. But the score didn't stay that way for long. And it was all Matt's fault.

Halfway through the third quarter, Coach called for a handoff to Matt. It was second down, and the Panthers needed eight yards. They had made a strong drive upfield, working their way to the North Colby 35-yard line. But when Matt got the call, he wasn't thinking about just getting the eight yards needed for a first down. He wanted to go the whole 35, for the big touchdown.

I've got to score, I've got to score, Matt thought, as he squatted down. He was so nervous that he wondered if he'd be able to move at all.

"Hut! Hut!"

Matt sprang forward and took the ball from Jesse in a perfect handoff. He looked for the hole in the defense, but didn't see any. So he turned back and ran across the field toward the sideline, only the defense was closing in on him, fast. He was about to make his break upfield when his legs seemed to freeze—and a second later the North Colby defense slammed into him. As Matt was falling to the ground, he felt the ball break free of his hands. Another fumble!

North Colby recovered, and ran the ball for a touchdown.

Meanwhile, Matt lay on the ground, wishing he could disappear.

North Colby made the extra point to tie the score at 7–7.

Late in the fourth quarter, Jesse threw a beautiful pass to Chuck McPhee. Chuck caught the ball at the North Colby 20, and then made a great run across the gridiron and into the corner of the end zone.

When the referee raised his arms to signal the touchdown, the Alden bleachers went nuts. The game's final buzzer sounded, with Alden beating North Colby 14–7. It was Alden's first victory.

After the game, the whole team was cheering in the locker room. The Panthers' year was off to a fantastic start! There were high fives and congratulations being passed all around.

But Matt didn't join in.

"All right!" Woody said, coming up to Matt, and slapping him on the back. "The Panthers rule!"

Matt just shrugged.

"Aw, come on, Matt," Woody said. "Forget about your fumble. We *all* make mistakes. The important thing is that the *team* won."

"I guess so," Matt said.

Matt realized that Woody was right—the important thing was that the Panthers had won. Somehow, though, he didn't think his dad would feel that way.

Mr. Greene was sitting in the family room when Matt walked in later that afternoon. He called Matt over and pointed to a chair. Matt sat down. Then Mr. Greene turned on the TV and suddenly Matt saw the Alden field, and all the Panthers in blue and gold.

41

"You had a good first half, son," Mr. Greene began. "You moved the ball well, and even gave a few good head fakes. Your blocking wasn't the greatest; still, it was okay. But in the second half, you fell apart. Now I want you to watch yourself making that fumble. And then I want you to tell me exactly what you did wrong."

Matt felt a little sick to his stomach as he watched himself lose control of the ball, and then watched North Colby recover and run the ball for their only touchdown. He looked so slow, and so *bad!*

"I guess I didn't tuck the ball in close enough to my body," Matt said.

"That's one thing," Mr. Greene said. "You made a lot of other mistakes, too."

His dad made him watch the fumble twice more, each time explaining another thing Matt had done wrong. He told Matt that he had to take football more seriously, that he had to sleep, eat, and breathe football.

But Matt was beginning to hate football.

5

Sunday, Matt couldn't wait to spend a whole day without so much as touching a football. He was actually looking forward to doing his homework, just to get his mind off yesterday's game. His dad would probably make him watch the afternoon pro game on TV, but that was okay. As long as he was only *watching* football, then at least he couldn't make a fool of himself in front of his father.

Matt was in his bedroom, working on his math, when Mr. Greene opened the door.

"Josh just phoned," Mr. Greene said. "He said that a bunch of guys from the team are meeting over at Danahy's Park, for a pickup game."

"But I'm doing my homework, Dad," Matt said, his heart sinking. "I've got ten math problems due tomorrow."

"Those ten math problems can wait until it's dark outside," Mr. Greene answered. "But while it's still light, you've got to practice."

"But, Dad . . ." Matt began.

"No *but*s," Mr. Greene said. "After your fumble yesterday, I would think you'd *want* to play some more. You do want to improve, don't you?"

"Yes, sir," Matt said, putting down his pencil.

Dad's right, Matt thought, as he ran toward Danahy's Park. *I had a bad game yesterday, and I've got to improve. I've got to show Dad what I can do.*

By the time Matt got to Danahy's Park, the sides had already been chosen, and everyone was tossing footballs and horsing around. The teams were Josh, Dave McShea, Bruce Judge, and John DeLuca against Jesse, Woody, Duke Duquette, and Dan Caner. But nobody seemed to want Matt on their team.

"Why don't *you* guys take him," Josh said.

"It was your idea to call him, Josh," Jesse answered. "I say *you* get him."

Matt couldn't believe it. Here he was with his best friends, and nobody even wanted him on their team! Wasn't he the running back? Wasn't he Big Bill Greene's son?

Who cares? Matt thought. *I didn't come here to have a party. I came here to practice football.*

Finally, Josh agreed to take Matt on his team.

"Are we playing tackle or touch?" Woody asked, as the boys gathered in the center of the field.

"Coach told us that we should only play touch, if we're not in full pads," Dave said.

"He's probably right," Bruce responded. "We can't afford to have any injuries in a pickup game."

"Okay, two-hand tag," Woody said.

"Forget it!" Matt said. "What are we? A bunch of sissies? If we're here to play, then we've got to play hard. And that means tackling."

After a few minutes Matt won the argument, and the two teams lined up to play a game of full-contact football.

"Let's use my special football," Josh said, picking up the ball that Big Bill had given to him a week before. "It'll help us play like pros, since it's got Big Bill's autograph on it."

The goals were imaginary lines between huge oak trees. Matt punted the ball high into the air for the kickoff, and then charged forward for the tackle. He knew that Coach was right: they shouldn't play tackle football without pads. But Matt could just imagine what his father would say about a game of *touch* football.

Dan Caner caught the kickoff and started upfield, but Dave McShea tackled him at about the 30-yard line.

"What kind of sissy tackle was *that?*" Matt said to Dave in the huddle.

"Loosen up, Matt," Josh answered. "We're out here to have fun, not break bones."

The two teams lined up at the line of scrimmage. Matt was covering Bruce Judge, who was usually a lineman and not very fast. Matt ran slow and let Bruce get open—and Jesse threw a long ball to Bruce.

It was just what Matt had planned. As soon as Matt saw the ball leave Jesse's hand, he charged forward, overtook Bruce, and leaped in the air to make the interception. Then he took off along the sideline toward the two far oak trees.

When Woody rushed over to make the tackle, Matt straight-armed him, and Woody tumbled to the ground, struggling to catch his breath. Matt ran across the goal line and spiked the ball into the grass.

He turned around with his arms held high, expecting to be mobbed by his teammates, but no one was there.

Instead, everyone was standing over Woody, asking him if he was okay. He was all right, just a little shaken up by Matt's straight-arm. Woody got up slowly, sent Matt an angry look, and walked back to receive the kickoff.

"Take it easy, Matt," Josh said. "This isn't a championship game or anything."

All Matt could think of was how proud his father would have been to see him score his touchdown.

Jesse fielded the kickoff and started running toward the goal line. Matt zeroed in on him and rushed toward him as fast as he could. At the last minute, he dived forward and tackled Jesse around the waist.

"Ow, ow!" Jesse called out, holding his wrist.

"What happened?" Josh said, rushing up. "Are you okay?"

"Matt came down on my wrist," Jesse said, his face screwed up with pain.

"Nice going, Mr. Tackle," Josh said to Matt. Josh's face was turning red with anger. "Now you've hurt our quarterback."

"Oh, come on, you guys," Matt said. "Players always get injured."

"Why don't you just cool it, Matt," Woody said, as he helped Jesse to his feet. "Your dad's not here. You don't have to impress anybody."

"Leave my dad out of this," Matt shouted.

"Why should we?" Josh asked. "Don't you think we know why you've been such a total *jerk* since football started?"

"A jerk?" Matt said. "Am I a jerk just because I take football seriously?"

"Maybe you could talk that way if you were a superstar, like your dad," Josh said, pushing Matt a little. "But the fact is, all you did in yesterday's game was *fumble*."

"I rushed for thirty-seven yards, for your information," Matt said, stepping up closer to Josh, so their noses almost touched.

"Big deal," Josh said, stepping closer in to Matt. "It was *your* fumble that gave North Colby their only touchdown."

"Oh, yeah?" Matt said, giving Josh a little push in the chest.

"Yeah," Josh answered, pushing Matt right back. "And I've had enough of you."

Josh pushed Matt again, and Matt was just about ready to throw a punch when everyone rushed in to break it up.

"I think we better call it a day," Woody said, leading Josh away.

Josh turned and walked off the field with Woody. Jesse gave Matt a cold stare as he walked away, holding his wrist. In a minute, everyone was gone. The game was over before it had even begun.

Matt couldn't believe what had just happened. He had almost had a fight with his best friend.

I can't help it if those guys are a bunch of babies, Matt thought, as he walked over to Big Bill's Goalpost. *If they can't handle hard-hitting football, then they shouldn't be playing.*

Matt was surprised to see his father standing at the door.

"Done so soon?" Mr. Greene asked.

"Those guys wanted to play two-hand touch," Matt said.

"When I was your age, I played pickup football games with guys twice as big as I was . . . with no pads," Mr. Greene said.

"I know," Matt said. He sat down in a corner of the restaurant and looked up at the big-screen TV. In the video, his father was getting a pitchout. Big Bill Greene faked to the left, and then cut into a hole that had opened in the defense. After a few stutter steps and a perfect head fake, he hit the open field and sprinted for a 20-yard touchdown.

Matt remembered how he and Josh used to spend hours in the backyard, tossing the football and pretending they were in the NFL. They had spent most of their time laughing and fooling around. Sometimes Josh could get Matt laughing so hard that he would fall over.

Just then Josh walked into the restaurant, holding a football.

"I thought I'd find you here," Josh said.

The two friends looked at each other without smiling.

"I came here to give you this football back," Josh said. He put the football on the table. It was the one with Big Bill's autograph. "We used to be friends. But you've changed. I'm tired of hearing that I'm a baby, just because I like to have some fun."

Matt looked at the football on the table. His saw his father's autograph scrawled across the leather.

Josh reached down into his gym bag and pulled out two other balls.

"These are the balls your dad gave to Woody and Jesse," Josh continued. "They wanted me to give them to you. We're all sick of your attitude. And we're sick and tired of trying to be your friends."

With that, Josh turned around and left.

Matt sat there, stunned, looking at the three foot-balls on the table. Josh, Woody, and Jesse were his best friends—or used to be. But now everything had exploded into a million pieces.

Mr. Greene came back to Matt's table. "Why do you have these footballs?" he asked. "I thought I gave those to your friends."

"Oh . . . um," Matt answered, "they want you to write some more things on the balls."

6

On Tuesday the Panthers were scrimmaging to get ready for their next game at Williamsport.

Jesse got the snap, turned, and slammed the ball so hard into Matt's stomach that Matt lost his breath. Matt kept his grip on the handoff, and struggled through a hole in the defense. John DeLuca, an Alden defenseman, reached out and grabbed him by the ankle. Matt tried twisting to break free. Coach was about to blow the whistle and call the play dead, when Woody came flying through the air and crashed into Matt's side. Matt slammed to the ground and Woody landed right on top of him.

"Did I tackle you a little hard?" Woody said as he laid on top of Matt. "Or did you want to play touch football?"

Matt was too busy gasping for air to answer.

Coach blew the whistle and ran out to Matt, who lay on his back in the grass.

"You okay, Matt?" he said, kneeling down.

"I'll be fine," Matt answered.

"Hey, Woody," Coach said, as he helped Matt to his feet. "Take it easy out there. This is only a scrimmage."

The next call was for another handoff to Matt. Luckily, Jesse's wrist was okay, but Jesse was still angry at Matt about Sunday's pickup game. Matt knew that Jesse was slamming the ball into his stomach on purpose. But on this handoff, Matt was determined to be prepared.

He crouched down in the three-point stance and rushed forward, flexing his stomach muscles like someone was about to hit him. Jesse turned and slammed the ball into Matt's stomach even harder than before. This time Matt didn't lose his breath.

In fact, he was so angry at all his friends—his *ex*-friends—that he felt he would be able to break through *any* tackle and score a touchdown.

Woody and John DeLuca didn't let that happen. They slammed into Matt at the same time, full force. John cut Matt's legs out from under him, while Woody caught Matt in the shoulder, sending him flipping into the air, as the ball flew free. Matt's legs spun around like the spokes of a wheel, and he landed hard on his side. Coach blew the whistle before the defense could return the fumble.

"You okay, Matt?" Coach said, as Matt struggled to his feet and glared at Jesse and Woody.

Matt only nodded. Even through the helmet, Coach could see the anger in Matt's eyes.

Matt gave Jesse a shove as they fell into the huddle. When Jesse shoved Matt back, Coach blew the whistle again.

"What's wrong with you guys?" Coach shouted. "We're on the same team, remember? Now let's stop acting like children and get some practicing done."

But the rest of the scrimmage was exactly the same. It seemed like everyone was trying to smash Matt, and team spirit was at an all-time low.

Matt knew the team was trying to get even with him for last Sunday, but the more he tried to forget about it, the angrier he got. He began to block harder and harder, until he was nearly throwing himself at defensemen. Soon, the scrimmage started looking like a martial arts battle, with the hits getting harder and harder. Finally, Coach blew the whistle and called the practice early. He told his players they'd be better off saving the hard tackles for Williamsport.

Before the game on Saturday, Coach Wright had a few things to say to his team in the locker room.

"Listen up, men," Coach called out, rapping his clipboard against the lockers to get the team's attention. "We played a great game last weekend. I'm proud of each and every one of you. But Williamsport is a different team, and this time we don't have the home field advantage. So we have to be as psyched up for Williamsport as we were for North Colby. Right?"

"Right," a few voices said quietly.

"I didn't hear you?" Coach said.

"Right!" the whole team said in unison.

The whole team, that is, except for Matt. He was standing just outside the circle of players. Coach remembered the week's practices.

"I'll be honest with you, men," Coach continued. "I've noticed that our team spirit has been pretty low this week. We have to pull ourselves together and play as a *team*. That's the only way we'll win. Right?"

"Right!" everyone called out, except Matt.

"I didn't hear you!" Coach shouted.

"Right!!" everyone shouted back.

"All right, let's show them our stuff!" Coach called out.

He watched his players run out of the locker room and onto the field. Coach could tell that he had gotten most of the team psyched up, but he didn't know about Matt. He watched as Matt trotted behind his teammates, with his head hanging down. He knew that Matt was the reason for the Panthers' low spirit. And he suspected that Big Bill Greene was the reason for *Matt's* low spirit.

Coach hated to see a player as talented as Matt playing below his potential. If Matt didn't show some improvement by the end of this game, Coach knew he'd have to do something about it.

The day was perfect for football: cool crisp air, and a bright blue sky.

But Matt wished he could be anywhere else in the world than on a football field. It had been a miserable week. Not only were his ex-friends giving him the cold shoulder, but his dad was putting more pressure on him than ever. Matt glanced back into the bleachers, peppered mostly with Williamsport parents, and saw his father setting up the video camera.

I know I'm going to mess up today, Matt thought to himself.

And Matt was right. It seemed that the harder he tried, the more frustrated he got. He was so sure that he was going to play badly that his legs seemed to turn to ice every time he got the ball. Matt never gained more than two yards on a carry—and more often than not, he was tackled behind the line of scrimmage for a loss.

I'll never be good enough, he thought. *Never.*

The rest of the Panthers didn't let Matt's attitude bring them down. They played as if Matt weren't even there. During the first quarter, neither team made a big drive. Both defenses were playing so well that it looked like it was going to be a game of punts.

Things changed in the second quarter, when Josh ran a beautiful flag pattern and caught Jesse's pass for a 27-yard gain, putting the Panthers on the Williamsport 38-yard line. It was the most important drive of the game, and the crowd suddenly came to life. Matt could feel the new electricity in the air.

Coach Wright called in the play, and Jesse barked it out in the huddle.

"Thirty-eight, handoff left, on two. Break!"

Matt's heart beat nervously as he waited for the play to begin. He could tell that Jesse was still ticked off about his wrist—but he also knew that Jesse would never let something like that jeopardize a *real* conference game. Matt gazed forward, ready to leap into action.

"Hut! Hut!"

Matt saw Jesse turn and stuff the ball into his stomach. Matt clasped the ball and looked for his blockers. On this play, Josh was supposed to come over from the wide receiver position and block for him. Out of the corner of his eye, Matt could see Josh get knocked down. The hole that was supposed to open up in the Williamsport defense never appeared, and Matt went rushing into a wall of Williamsport jerseys. He only gained a yard.

"Come on, guys," Jesse said as they walked back to the huddle. "Let's not blow our big chance to score."

"Yeah, let's not blow it," Josh repeated, looking straight at Matt.

"Hey, *you* were supposed to block for me," Matt said to Josh. "If you had done your job, I'd be standing in the end zone now."

"In your dreams," Josh answered.

"Okay, enough of that," Jesse said. "Coach wants thirty-eight, pitchout right, on three."

Matt heard a few groans in the huddle, when the call for the next play went to him again. This time he'd show his team, and his dad, what he was made of.

Matt felt like he was breathing fire as he waited for the snap. He knew he had to make up some yardage on this play to give the Panthers a shot at a first down.

"Hut! Hut! Hut!"

Matt broke right, and saw Jesse turn and pitch the ball into his hands. Matt was supposed to break toward the sideline, and then cut upfield. Josh was running in front of him, and threw a beautiful block that opened up a hole, and Matt cut sharply through the hole—too sharply. His ankle slipped on the damp grass and he fell forward. A split second later, Matt felt two Williamsport players smash into his back to complete the tackle. He had gained only two more yards.

"I gave you a great block this time, and look what you did with it," Josh muttered as they walked back to the huddle.

"I slipped, okay?" Matt said.

It was getting serious now: third down, and seven

yards for a first down. At the 35-yard line, they were still too far out for a field goal. The Panthers *had* to get the first down.

"Forty-two, flag pattern right. Seventeen, post pattern left. Thirty-eight, play action. On two. Break!"

Play action meant that Jesse would fake a handoff to Matt, and Matt would then help block while Jesse faded back for the pass. The idea was to fool Williamsport into thinking that the Panthers were handing off.

Matt bounded forward, lifted his arms as if he were going to receive the handoff, and then barrelled forward toward the defense. He lost his footing again and fell. The lineman he was supposed to block went running right over him. When Matt looked up, he saw Jesse being sacked.

The Panthers had blown their first big drive of the game, and it was Matt's fault. The game wasn't lost, though. Later in the quarter Josh caught a 20-yard pass and ran it another 20 into the Willliamsport end zone. Jesse followed the touchdown with a quarterback option over the goal line to bring the score to 8–0. On their next possession, Williamsport drove the ball deep enough to get a field goal, and at the end of the first half the score was Alden 8, Williamsport 3.

As Alden was running back onto the field after the halftime break, Matt heard a familiar voice calling to him from the sidelines. Suddenly, his blood ran cold.

"Hey, Matt!" Mr. Greene called out. "I want to talk to you."

Matt dragged himself over to the fence. He knew he was about to get a *big* piece of his father's mind.

"Pull yourself together out there," Mr. Greene said. "I don't want to see you slipping down anymore. Your job is to score touchdowns. So get out there and do it!"

Matt turned around and trotted back to his team. He felt about two inches tall.

I'm not good enough for anyone, Matt thought, as the team hit the field. *I'm not good enough for Josh and Woody and Jesse. And I'm not good enough for Dad.*

Not surprisingly, Matt played even worse in the second half. The whole team was giving him the cold shoulder. Toward the end of the fourth quarter, Coach called for the halfback option. Matt decided it was time to score a touchdown.

The Panthers were on the Williamsport 33-yard line. It was third down, and Alden needed only two yards for the first down.

Jesse chanted the count.

"Hut! Hut! Hut!"

The Panthers went into action. Jesse pitched the ball out to Matt, and Josh sprinted out in a post pattern. Matt saw Josh outrun his defender and lift his hand to get the pass. But Matt had decided it was time for him to run. He turned toward the line of scrimmage and sprinted desperately toward a hole in the defense.

The Williamsport safety cut across the field and flew into Matt's side in a beautiful tackle. Matt could feel the ball jar loose and slip from his hands just before he hit the ground. He tried to scramble to recover the fumble, but he was too late. A Williamsport lineman picked it up, and outran Jesse for a touchdown.

Matt walked back to the sidelines with his head down.

"Nice work, superstar," Josh said with a sneer, on the sidelines. "Thanks to you, we're behind by two points."

"Why don't you just shut up, Josh," Matt said, as he turned around and walked away.

There were only two minutes left in the game, and the score was Williamsport 10, Alden 8. Duke Duquette received the kickoff for Alden and ran it back to the 35. Then, luckily, Jesse connected with Josh on a beautiful bomb that brought Alden within field goal distance. With only 30 seconds left on the clock, Alden's field goal kicker, John DeLuca, kicked the ball through the uprights, and what few Alden fans were there went crazy.

Alden had won, 11–10.

On the way home to Cranbrook, Coach Wright noticed that Matt was sitting all by himself in the back of the bus. Everybody else was up in the front, laughing and cheering and slapping each other on the back. Coach knew that if he didn't solve the Matt Greene problem—and solve it fast—the Panthers would fall apart.

Matt had played a terrible game, rushing for only 16 yards. Coach figured that a kid with Matt's talent should be rushing for at least 70 yards a game, maybe 80.

He decided that it was time to have a little chat with Matt—especially after he overheard the boys talking on the bus.

"I'm just pretending like Matt isn't even on the team anymore," Josh said.

"We don't need him anyway," Jesse responded. "We've won two games already, and Matt hasn't helped a bit."

"Yeah," Josh said. "Who needs Big Bill Greene's son?"

7

Later that same afternoon, Coach Wright stood in the parking lot at Alden Junior High, congratulating his players as they stepped off the bus. After everyone else on the team had left to celebrate the victory at Pete's Pizza, Matt walked slowly down the bus steps. He looked glum as he carried his gym bag and helmet.

"Hey, there, Matt," Coach Wright said, leaning against the bus. "You got a minute?"

Matt didn't even look up at Coach.

"I guess so," Matt said quietly.

"Good," Coach said putting his arm around Matt's shoulders. "Let's go into my office and have a little chat."

Coach led Matt into the gym and over to a small office, with windows that looked out on a patch of woods. The office was filled with old photographs of football teams, a few old helmets, and some banners from the college where Big Bill and Coach Wright had played ball. Coach asked Matt to sit down.

"Matt, I'm going to be honest with you," Coach began. "I'm worried about you. You haven't been playing up to your potential. In fact, you're playing at about one-*fourth* of your potential. And that's *not* very good."

Matt nodded.

"You're one of the most talented young running backs I've ever coached, and I want to see you play as well as you can," Coach said. "But you have to let me help you."

"I'm just not good enough, Coach," Matt said. "No matter how hard I try, I only seem to screw up."

"Have you ever thought that maybe you're trying *too* hard?" Coach asked.

"My dad always says you can *never* try too hard," Matt answered. "He always says football has to be

66

your whole life. He says that you have to eat, sleep, and breathe football."

"Do you believe him?" Coach asked.

"I guess so," Matt said. "He *is* Big Bill Greene, you know. He *is* one of the greatest running backs in NFL history."

"I want to show you something," Coach said, placing a photograph in Matt's hand. "This is a picture of the college team that your father and I were on. Can you find your dad?"

"He's the one over in the corner, all by himself," Matt answered, pointing to the old photograph of Big Bill Greene.

"That's right," Coach answered. "Do you know why your dad is standing all alone, with nobody around him?"

"No."

"Because all your father did was eat, sleep, and breathe football," Coach said. "Sure, he was a great player. But nobody could be his friend, because he took everything too seriously. And football *has* to be fun, Matt—but your dad didn't understand that. He just worked and worked, and practiced and practiced."

Matt just stared at the picture, blinking his eyes and thinking.

"What about you, Matt?" Coach said. "Are you enjoying the season? Are you having fun with Josh, and Woody, and Jesse?"

"Not really," Matt said, looking up at Coach. "We're not friends anymore."

Coach just nodded and looked at Matt.

"Thanks for showing me that picture, Coach," Matt said, standing up.

"I thought you needed to see it. Now go on home and think about what we've said today."

As Matt walked home along the streets of Cranbrook, he thought long and hard about what Coach Wright had said. He didn't want to end up without any friends—like his father had. He wanted to make up with Josh, and Woody, and Jesse. He wanted to laugh and fool around like they always had. And he knew that if he started taking his football a little less seriously, he would probably turn out to be the best player on the Panthers.

He felt great walking home—like a huge weight had been lifted from his shoulders. Everything was going to be fine after all. He would get his friends back . . . *and* be the star player of the Alden football team.

But Matt had forgotten about one thing: his dad.

"Matt?" Mr. Greene called out, as soon as Matt came through the door. "Can you come here, please? I have a few things to say to you."

Matt walked into the family room. His dad was sitting on the sofa with an angry expression on his face. Matt felt his heart sink. Suddenly, he didn't feel as great as he had a minute before.

"I'm disappointed in you, son," Mr. Greene began. "You played like a quitter in the game today."

Matt looked down at the ground.

"Sit down and watch yourself," Mr. Greene said, turning on the TV. But Matt could barely keep his eyes on the screen. Just once, he wanted to hear his father say that he was actually *proud* of him.

On Monday Matt saw all his friends sitting together in the lunchroom, laughing and telling jokes. He watched Josh make a funny face that made Jesse laugh so hard that he almost choked on his food. Matt really missed his friends. The last thing in the world he wanted was to end up like his dad, all alone in the far corner of the team photograph. Right then, Matt decided it was time to make up with Josh, Woody, and Jesse.

It wasn't as easy as Matt had hoped. The minute he sat down at the table and opened up his lunch bag, all of his friends stopped laughing. Suddenly everybody grew very quiet. "Hey, guys," Matt said, trying to smile. "You played a great game yesterday."

Nobody said anything. Josh didn't even look up at him. His friends just ate their sandwiches in silence.

"So are you getting psyched up for our game against Lincoln this week?" Matt asked.

Nobody answered.

"Hey, come on," Matt said, getting a little angry. "I'm just trying to be nice."

"Oh, yeah?" Josh said finally. "Well why don't you stop trying to be nice, and just be *Matt*?"

With that, Josh and Woody and Jesse all got up and moved to a different table.

Suddenly, Matt didn't feel very hungry anymore.

8

Alden faced their rival, Lincoln, on Friday. From the kickoff, it was a fierce and even battle. During the whole first quarter, neither team was able to put together a successful drive. The Alden and Lincoln defenses were both tough, and they were stopping the offenses cold.

Luckily, the Panthers' punter, Dan Caner, was having a great day. Early in the second quarter, Dan punted the ball a full 40 yards. Matt watched in awe as the ball went sailing over the receiver's head and

bounced out of bounds at the Lincoln 15-yard line—
a perfect punt. Woody led the Alden defense, only
letting Lincoln advance a few inches before forcing
them to punt again, from deep in their own territory.

The Lincoln punter scuffed the ball and Matt
caught it on the bounce, running it back past mid-
field and into Lincoln territory. He gave a nice head
fake, spun out of a tackle, and then turned on the
speed along the sideline. Matt could see the goal line
up ahead, and as he ran he could almost feel the
exhilaration of his first *real* touchdown.

Just then, Matt was knocked out of bounds by a
fast Lincoln defender. Even though he didn't score,
he *had* broken the slump that the offense had been
in—and he *had* carried the ball all the way to the
Lincoln 19-yard line. As he ran back toward the huddle, listening to the cheers of the Alden fans, Matt
expected to get a round of high fives from the team.
Instead, everyone—Josh, Jesse, Dave, Bruce—pre-
tended that he didn't even exist. The boys didn't say
a word to him in the huddle, except when Jesse called
out the play.

"Thirty-eight, screen pass right, on three. Break!"

As Matt settled into the three-point position, he
felt his excitement over his great punt return disappear. It seemed that no matter how well he played,

his teammates still gave him the cold shoulder. Matt could tell the team's spirit was at an all-time low—and suddenly, his spirit was lower than ever, too.

"Hut! Hut! Hut!"

Matt ran forward, crossed the line of scrimmage, and turned to get the screen pass. Jesse's throw was wobbly, like a wounded duck, and Matt couldn't hold onto it. After the ref blew the ball dead, Matt walked back to the huddle knowing that he *should* have caught the ball.

The next play was a pass attempt, but Jesse overthrew the receiver, and the Panthers gathered in the huddle at third down and ten. Matt got the call for a handoff.

At the snap, Matt burst forward, grabbed the ball from Jesse, and cut sharply toward a hole in the defense. He moved like a natural running back, faking and dodging, spinning out of one tackle, leaping over fallen players, until he was finally brought down just three yards shy of the first down. The crowd cheered him as he rose from the tackle.

It was another beautiful run, but no one on the team congratulated him. As Matt jogged back to the huddle, he only hoped that Coach would let him gun for the first down. Surely *that* would get the Panthers back on his side. Matt glanced over to the sidelines and saw Coach waving everyone off the field. Matt knew what that meant: the Panthers were going for the field goal, and three easy points.

John DeLuca's kick was way left, and the Panthers had wasted their first scoring opportunity of the game. When the first half ended, the score was still 0–0.

As the Panthers were walking back from the locker rooms for the second half, Matt heard his father call him over to the sidelines. "How much longer are you guys going to punt?" Mr. Greene said. "All I've seen this game is punt, punt, punt. It's *your* job to make sure that the offense moves up field."

"Yes, sir," Matt answered.

"Get out there and do *whatever* it takes for you to score," Mr. Greene added.

Matt walked back to the sidelines, and remembered his talk with Coach Wright. He now knew that he would never play well as long as he was trying to live up to his father. Still, he wanted to make his father proud.

I'll just have to do it on my own, Matt thought, as the teams lined up for the kickoff. *Even if my friends hate me.*

On Alden's first possession, Matt was ready to

play—too ready. He jumped the count and the Panthers were penalized for illegal motion.

"Listen for the count, Greene," Jesse scowled at Matt.

"Yeah, hotshot," Josh said. "Are you trying to make us look bad?"

"I'm sorry if I made a mistake," Matt said, in the huddle. "I'm not perfect."

"Sorry isn't good enough," Josh answered.

Luckily, Dan Caner kicked a beautiful punt and the Panthers got out of trouble. But in the middle of the fourth quarter, Dan hurt his ankle on a defensive play and Alden lost its star punter.

The next time Alden needed to punt, Coach called Matt over.

"Matt," Coach said. "I want you to punt. We're way back on our own twenty-five, so this is a very important kick."

Matt was a good punter—that is, whenever he and Josh used to kick the ball around in the backyard. But he had never punted in a real game situation before.

Time was running out in the game. When was he going to score a touchdown?

I've got it, Matt thought, as he walked out to the

field to punt. *I've got to score a touchdown, and this is my last chance.*

Matt's heart was pounding like crazy as he received the snap. He knew he was taking a huge chance . . . but he would never score a touchdown by punting.

So Matt faked the punt, tucked the ball under his arm, and took off sprinting upfield.

I can't believe I'm doing this, Matt thought as he dodged a tackle. *I have to run 75 yards to get a touchdown.*

He didn't make it. The Alden offense was as surprised by Matt's play as Lincoln was. In the confusion, Josh accidentally knocked into Matt, and the ball flew out of Matt's hands.

I don't believe it, Matt thought desperately, as he watched the ball bounce toward a group of Lincoln players. *Why can't anything go right?*

Lincoln recovered the fumble and ran it in for the first touchdown of the game—and Alden didn't have a chance to come back. There were only three minutes left before the final buzzer. When the game ended, the final score was Lincoln 7, Alden 0.

"Thanks for losing the game for us," Jesse said as he walked by Matt toward the lockers.

"I don't care who your dad is, you still stink," Duke Duquette said.

"Hey, thanks a lot for making me look bad," Josh said.

"But *you* ran into *me*," Matt said.

"What kind of stupid idea did you have to run the ball, anyway?" Josh asked. "I'm sure your dad was very impressed."

Right then, Matt felt like running away and never coming back to Alden Junior High.

Coach knew that Matt had made a huge mistake by running his own play, against the coach's orders. And he knew that Big Bill would be right to say that Matt had let everyone down. Coach also knew that Matt would never change unless his father changed, too.

When Matt left for the locker room, Coach Wright walked over to his old college teammate.

"Hello, Bill," Coach Wright said. "Can I meet you later, maybe for dinner, to talk about Matt?"

"Why not?" Big Bill said. "Why don't you come over to my restaurant and I'll treat you to a steak. And we can have a good long talk."

When Coach Wright showed up at Big Bill's Goalpost, he couldn't believe his eyes. *No wonder Matt is under so much pressure,* Coach thought as he looked around. *Everywhere he looks it's football, football, football.*

Big Bill greeted Coach and the two men sat down at a table in the corner.

"Bill," Coach began, "I'm worried about Matt."

"So am I," Big Bill said. "I thought the boy had some guts, some talent, but I guess he doesn't."

"Listen," Coach said. "Matt is one of the most talented players I've ever coached. His moves are as natural as a tiger. But the problem is, he's playing way under his potential. And I think I know how we can help him."

"I know how we can help him, too," Big Bill said. "He needs to practice more. He needs to get serious about his football."

"I disagree," Coach said. "In fact, he needs to get *less* serious about his football. Listen, I'll be honest with you, Bill. You're putting an awful lot of pressure on Matt. Don't you understand how hard it is for Matt to live in your shadow? He's always trying to prove that he's good enough for you. In fact, he's been trying so hard that his game is getting *worse*. Not to mention that he's losing his friends."

Big Bill Greene didn't know what to say. He sat quietly, thinking.

"Bill, you're the only one who can turn Matt around," Coach Wright said.

"I have been pretty hard on Matt, haven't I?" Big Bill said. "But he has so much more talent than I ever did. I had to work and work to play as well as I did. But I can tell that Matt is a natural."

"Have you ever told him that?" Coach asked. "Have you ever told him how much talent you think he has?"

"No," Big Bill said. "Maybe it's time I did."

But Big Bill didn't tell Matt soon enough.

9

"Listen up, Panthers," Coach Wright said at practice on Monday. "We had a tough loss on Friday, but let's put it behind us, and move on."

Coach led the team over to the tires, to work on quickstepping and agility.

"We have all the talent we need to win the conference championship," Coach said. "But what we need is a little more team spirit."

"What we need is a new running back," Josh whispered to Jesse.

"No kidding," Jesse answered. "Someone who won't lose the whole game just because he wants to show off."

"We can't practice team spirit," Coach continued. "What we *can* do is practice agility. And we can practice blocking and running and passing. Now let's do some tires, men!"

Coach clapped his hands and the Panthers fell into line. Woody went in first, quickstepping into each tire. Josh went next, and then Bruce Judge, and then Jesse. Matt was at the end of the line.

Team spirit? Matt thought, as he watched his teammates run the tires. *How can I have any team spirit when everybody hates me?*

Matt's turn came to run the tires, and he started quickstepping. His feet moving easily through the tires. Whenever Matt sprinted, or did agility drills, it was easy to see how talented he was. His strong legs pumped like pistons, up and down with incredible speed. But Matt was running so fast that he caught his foot in the last tire and went flying into the dirt.

"What's wrong, hotshot?" Josh said with a little sneer, as Matt got up and brushed himself off. "I thought Big Bill's son was supposed to be the star of the team. Seems to me he can't even run the tires."

Matt didn't say a word, but he was sick of Josh's attitude. Wasn't it bad enough that Josh wasn't his best friend anymore? Did he have to heckle Matt so much?

Coach called the boys over for a scrimmage game, saying that they needed to work on their offense. Matt knew that Coach was right: if the Panthers ever got their offense together, they had a shot at the conference championship.

As he walked out to the field, Matt glanced up into the bleachers. His father was not there, and Matt sighed with relief. Maybe now he could relax enough to actually get down to the business of playing football.

Coach started the offense on their own 20-yard line, calling for a handoff to Matt. Matt crouched down and raised his head, staring forward at Jesse's back and waiting for the snap. When Bruce snapped the ball into Jesse's hands, Matt rushed forward and took the handoff. He broke left, toward a small hole in the Panther defense, and twisted out of Woody's tackle. Suddenly his legs felt fast and strong, and Matt knew that nobody could tackle him. He dodged left toward the sideline, sinking his shoulder pad into Duke's chest and knocking him on his back. He turned up the left sideline and saw another defender rushing across the field toward him. All Matt did was change his speed for a split second, and the defender went tumbling past him and out of bounds. Then Matt cut sharply right and sprinted toward the end zone.

The only defender near him was too far back to have a chance. When Matt Greene turned on the speed, no one on the team—maybe no one in the entire conference—could catch him.

He crossed the goal line, and then jogged back toward the huddle holding the ball. It was an incredible 80-yard run, but Matt knew that his teammates wouldn't even give him a single high five.

"Why don't you start running like that during games?" Josh muttered. "It doesn't matter if you run well at practice, if you keep losing games for us."

"Hey, Josh," Matt said. "*You* ran into me in the game yesterday. *You* knocked the ball out of my hands. That's why I fumbled."

"Give me a break," Josh shouted, his face turning bright red. "You lost the game for us and you know it. If you lose *another* game, we won't have a chance at the championship."

The two boys were standing up close to each other. Matt was much bigger than Josh, so he looked down into Josh's face. But Josh was a fireball. When he got mad and wanted to fight, he didn't care how big the other guy was.

"In fact, I've had just about enough of your lousy attitude," Josh said, pushing Matt in the chest.

"Oh, yeah?" Matt said, pushing Josh back. "Your attitude is worse than mine!"

Josh pushed Matt in the chest again, and then Matt pushed Josh a little harder. Suddenly Josh took a swing and hit Matt in the stomach. Matt had the wind knocked out of him, but he swung his fist anyway and hit Josh right back in the stomach. Then the two boys started wrestling, and a second later the whole Alden team was yelling and screaming and trying to pull them apart.

Finally Coach Wright ran up and blew his whistle—and everyone shut up. Matt and Josh stood next to each other, looking at the coach like a couple of criminals.

"Do you see what I mean by team spirit?" Coach yelled angrily. "Now we're even starting to fight *ourselves*. I've had enough of this. Everybody hit the showers. Except Josh and Matt."

The whole team walked slowly toward the lockers, leaving Matt and Josh behind. Coach Wright asked them what had happened, but neither boy would say anything. Still, Coach had a pretty good idea what the problem was.

Big Bill had better talk with Matt soon, he thought. *Before things get completely out of hand.*

When Matt got home after practice, he went straight up into his room and flopped down on his bed. He couldn't believe he had actually *hit* Josh. Josh Bank! The guy who had been his best friend for so many years!

Just then Matt heard his father knock on his door.

Mr. Greene opened the door and walked into Matt's room. "Coach Wright just called me," Mr. Greene began, sitting down on the bed with Matt. "He told me about your fight with Josh. And I want you to know that I'm sorry."

Matt didn't know what to think. Why was his dad apologizing to *him?*

"Matt," Mr. Greene said, putting his hand on his son's shoulder. "I'm afraid I've been the cause of all your problems. I've been putting too much pressure on you to be the best. Do you know *why* I've been doing it?"

Matt lifted his head from his pillow and looked at his dad.

"I did it because you have so much talent," Mr. Greene said. "I did it because you have more talent than I *ever* had." Matt couldn't believe his ears. Was his father telling him that he, Matt, was *better* than his dad?

"Matt, the only way you'll ever play up to your potential is if you relax on the field and just enjoy playing the game," Mr. Greene said.

Matt stared.

"And don't ever neglect your friends," Mr. Greene continued. "Your friends—Josh and Woody and Jesse—should always be a part of your life. Now I'm not going to give you any orders, but I think you should make up with those guys. And with the whole team, too."

"I think so, too," Matt said.

"And Matt," Mr. Greene said, looking his son in the eyes. "This is the most important thing of all. I want you to know how proud I am of you."

10

Matt went to school the next day ready to apologize to Josh and everyone else. He knew it wouldn't be easy, but now that he knew his father was proud of him, Matt felt like he could do anything in the world.

Matt saw Josh in the lunchroom. Josh was sitting by himself, waiting for Woody and Jesse to show up. Matt's heart was beating like crazy as he walked toward his old best friend.

Josh saw Matt coming and gave him a cold stare.

"Truce!" Matt said, smiling and holding up his hand.

"Forget it, Matt," Josh said. "I don't have anything to say to you. And if you want to fight, I'll meet you outside after lunch."

"Josh," Matt said, looking down at the table. "I owe you an apology. I know I've been a real jerk lately, and I'm sorry."

Josh looked surprised. "You know what, Matt?" he said, with a little smile. "You're *right*. You *have* been acting like a real jerk lately."

Matt could see that Josh was starting to loosen up a little.

"I had a long talk with my dad last night, and things are going to change," Matt said.

"I sure hope so," Josh said, taking a big bite of his sandwich.

"I just hope the team will give me a second chance," Matt said with a big smile. "You know, if we can get our spirit up, I don't think there's a team in the conference that could beat us!"

"Not even Bradley?" Josh asked.

"Bradley's got a great team," Matt conceded. "But I think we can knock them out."

"Speaking of knocking people out . . ." Josh said,

rubbing his stomach where Matt had punched him. "Why don't we knock out the Bradley defense next time?"

"Deal!" Matt said. "Hey, I brought something for you."

Matt reached down into his knapsack and pulled out a brand-new professional football. He handed it to Josh. "And don't worry, Josh, my dad didn't autograph it," Matt said. "It's completely new."

Josh smiled and threw the ball into the air a few times, like he was thinking about something. Matt had seen that expression a thousand times before. He could tell that Josh was cooking up some sort of crazy plan.

"Go out for a bomb," Josh said, standing up from the lunch table.

"A bomb?" Matt said. "In the lunchroom?"

"Exactly," Josh said, smiling. "Go deep, flag pattern, on two. Break!"

Matt looked over at the vice principal, who was sitting at a table reading a paper.

Who cares if we get in trouble, Matt thought.

Josh called out the cadence—"Hut! Hut!"—and Matt went sprinting through the lunch tables, way over toward the far end, near the milk line. Josh

89

faded back and threw a long beautiful spiral pass. The ball sailed up close to the ceiling, and suddenly everybody in the lunchroom got quiet.

Matt looked back and saw the ball coming high across the tables. It was a perfect pass. All Matt did was open up his arms and catch the ball.

"Touchdown!!" Matt held up the ball and the entire lunchroom broke into applause.

"What happened?" the vice principal called out, looking up from his paper with a startled expression. "Why is everybody clapping?"

But no one told him a thing. Matt walked back toward Josh with the ball, and the two of them gave each other a high five.

"Great catch!" Josh said, slapping his friend's hand.

"Great pass!" Matt answered, smiling.

Just then Woody and Jesse came into the lunchroom, and saw Matt and Josh smiling and laughing together. They walked up to their two friends with confused looks on their faces.

"What's happened to you guys?" Woody asked, as he sat down at the table.

"What happened?" Josh asked. "Matt caught the bomb."

Woody and Jesse exchanged looks and shrugged.

They didn't have any idea what Josh was talking about. It didn't really matter. They were just glad that the Alden Panthers were going to be a team.

"I don't know what's gotten into you men," Coach Wright said at practice that afternoon. "But I sure do like it!"

It was by far the best practice the Panthers had ever had. Matt could feel the difference as soon as the team hit the field for a scrimmage game. For the first time all year, the Panthers had spirit.

"Okay, Matt," Jesse said in the huddle. "This next play is all yours. Pitchout left, on three. And let's show the defense what we're made of. Break!"

The offense hustled into position. As Jesse called off the numbers, the whole Panther team waited to explode into action.

"Hut! Hut! Hut!"

Matt sprang forward and to the left, and caught Jesse's pitchout. The fierce defense had broken through the line, and Woody was charging after Matt. Matt ducked and headed toward the sideline to avoid Woody's tackle. He turned and ran along the sideline, pumping his legs as fast as they'd go, with Woody in hot pursuit. Matt couldn't believe how fast Woody was running!

Woody let out a shout and dove forward, just barely gripping Matt's ankle. But it was enough to bring Matt down.

"Nice tackle," Matt said, as Woody gave Matt a hand to help him up.

"Excellent run," Woody answered. "I don't know how I ever caught you."

"No talking with the enemy," Josh said, walking up to his friends. "Woody, you leave our star running back alone."

The offense was now first and ten, on their own 40-yard line. Coach called for a pass play, and it was Matt's job to block for Jesse. Matt took out two defenders at once, giving Jesse plenty of time to throw. When Josh got open upfield, Jesse drew his arm back and hurled a perfect spiral pass that sped right into Josh's arms. Josh cut to his right and toward the goal line, gaining 18 yards before Chuck McPhee brought him down.

It was first and ten on the defense's 42. The Panther offense was working like a well-oiled machine, driving deep into the defense's territory. Coach called for a handoff to Matt, with Josh crossing over from the wide receiver position to block.

Matt snatched the handoff and cut right, hoping to make it through a hole in the line. As he cut,

Woody rushed in to plug the hole, and Matt realized he didn't have any way out. Just as Matt was ready to put his head down and drive into Woody for an extra yard, Josh came charging into Woody from the side, knocking him to the ground. Suddenly Matt had another hole, and he dodged his way through it. Matt continued to rush straight up the middle of the field, before being tackled at the 21-yard line. Another first down!

"Great run," Josh said, giving Matt a high five.

"I couldn't have done it without your killer block," Matt answered. "You really gave Woody a hit."

Now it was first and 10 from the 21, and Coach called for a screen pass to Matt. Matt could feel the excitement in the huddle—everyone wanted to score, and score *now*. Matt was ready to get down to business.

He sprinted out across the line of scrimmage, and turned to receive the pass. Jesse was looking right at him and waving him on. The play called for a short pass, but Jesse wanted Matt to go long. Matt broke upfield and saw Jesse throw just before he crossed the goal line. The pass was a little long, and Matt dived forward, catching the pass in his fingertips and landing on his stomach.

Touchdown! The whole offense, and even some of the defense, ran over to congratulate Matt.

"That's the way to play!" Coach Wright called out. "You guys are playing like champs."

Everyone let out a big cheer and gathered around Coach.

"Now that's the kind of spirit I like!" Coach continued. "And we're going to need all we can get next Wednesday when we play Bradley. They're the best team in the conference—or at least that's what they think. They think they've got the championship locked up. Do they?"

"*No!*" cried the Panthers.

"That's right!" Coach said, getting fired up. "Next week Bradley—then on to the championship!"

11

On Thursday, the Panthers gathered for their afternoon practice. The weather was getting colder, and there was even a little October frost on the lawns of Cranbrook. All the trees around the football field were on fire with autumn colors—red and yellow and orange. The boys could see their breath as they ran the tire drill and hit the blocking dummies.

Coach called them over to the goal line for a set of wind sprints. He blew the whistle and the team took off sprinting down the field, huffing and puffing in the cold air. As usual, Matt and Josh were ahead of the rest of the team, racing neck and neck. Matt could have turned on the afterburners for the last 15 yards, but instead he let his best friend pull ahead, and Josh beat him by three yards.

"Good race," Matt said, breathing hard and slapping Josh on the helmet.

"Thanks," Josh panted. "But this next one is all yours."

Matt thought he could see that sparkle in Josh's eyes—the sparkle that meant Josh was cooking up some plan. Matt didn't have time to worry about it, because Coach was already calling them up to the goal line for the second sprint.

"On your marks, get set . . . *go!*"

Matt and Josh pulled out early, running ten yards ahead of the rest of the team. They were still neck and neck with only 10 yards to go. Josh called out Matt's name and Matt glanced over. What he saw was Josh making his famous Godzilla-droid face. Matt burst into laughter. In fact, he started laughing so hard that he slowed down and Josh sped ahead and across the finish line. Matt crossed the finish line after Woody and Bruce and John and Dave. The only person Matt beat was Jesse—the slowest guy on the team. Matt was still laughing when he crossed the goal line.

"No fair, Josh!" Matt called out. "You didn't say anything about the Godzilla face!"

Josh slapped Matt on the shoulder pads. "I wanted to see if you've gotten your sense of humor back," Josh laughed. "And I'd say *maybe* you have."

"Okay, men, bring it in," Coach Wright called out. "Great practice. We're really playing like a *team*. Now the game against Bradley is next Wednesday, and I think we can beat those guys. But one way to make sure we beat them is to know as much about them as we can. Bradley has a game this afternoon, against Lincoln. I suggest that we go over there as a team, and do a little spying. What do you guys say?"

The whole team cheered. It would be good for the Alden Panthers to get a glimpse of their big opponents—and also, it would be a lot of fun.

The Bradley field was filled with spectators. All the Panthers sat together, in a big square section on the Bradley side. Woody was watching the game closely, trying to figure out how the Bradley offense worked. If he could understand their plays, then he would be able to defend against them.

Big Bill Greene had come along with the team after promising Matt not to give any football speeches. As it turned out, his advice was helpful. "See what the quarterback does, Woody?" Mr. Greene said, pointing down at the field. "He likes to use the play action. The play action is when he fakes like he's handing off, but he really goes back for the pass. So don't be fooled by it. Keep your eye on the ball at all times, or you may end up chasing a running back who doesn't even have the ball!"

"That's great!" Woody said. "Thanks, Mr. Greene."

"These guys don't look so tough," Jesse said. "Their quarterback hasn't completed a single pass over ten yards!"

"What do you think, Mr. Greene?" Josh asked.

"I think you guys can take Bradley," Mr. Greene answered. "But you'll have to be ready for a tough game."

Bradley ended up beating Lincoln 14–8. Lincoln was the only team that had beaten the Panthers so far that year—on the day last week when Matt faked the punt and ruined the game for Alden.

But all that seemed like a million years ago. In fact, it almost felt like the whole season was beginning again.

12

"Bradley is going to be overconfident," Coach Wright said, on the Wednesday of the next week. The whole team was gathered in the locker room, waiting for the game to start. "They think that because we lost to Lincoln, the team they just beat, the Panthers are going to roll over and die. Are we going to show them they're wrong?"

"Yes!" the whole team roared.

"That's right!" Coach Wright called out. "Now I want everyone to play this game like it was the championship game. We've gotten our spirit back. So let's use it! Let's get out there and show Bradley what the Panthers are made of!"

The team ran out of the locker room making banshee cries and waving their fists. Matt was ready to play—in fact, he had never wanted to play football so much in his life.

"Matt. Hey, Matt!" Mr. Greene called out, before the kickoff.

Matt heard his father's voice and ran over to the fence.

"Hey, son," Mr. Greene said, with a smile. "Just do your best. That's all I can ever ask of you."

"Thanks, Dad."

When Matt caught the kickoff and started up the field, he felt like nobody could stop him. The blocking up ahead was great, and a big hole opened up at around the 30-yard line. Matt faked a Bradley defenseman, cutting sharp and leaving him in the dust. He turned for the hole and broke two tackles, spinning around like a dancer. He faked out the safety by doing a set of stutter steps, just like he had seen his father do on the videos. Everyone in the bleachers was standing up to get a better view of his amazing run.

Matt spun free of the last tackler and saw a big

empty green space open up before him. He glanced over his shoulder to see Josh sprinting along behind him, to block.

"Go for it!" Josh called out. "Go for it!"

Matt turned on his afterburners and sprinted toward the Bradley goal.

I'm going to score! Matt thought as he approached the goal line.

Suddenly the Alden fans exploded with cheers, and Matt looked behind him to see the referee lift up his arms to signal a touchdown. Matt spiked the ball and then Josh came running up and jumped on top of him.

"Yeee-haah!" Josh cried.

A second later, the whole Alden offense was mobbing Matt and screaming. As they made their way back to the sideline, Matt heard the public address announcer's voice soaring over the crowd noise.

"Ladies and gentlemen," the voice said, "Matt Greene's eighty-six-yard kickoff return is an Alden Junior High record, beating the previous record of seventy-two yards set in 1956."

The crowd cheered louder.

"Great run," Coach Wright cried, slapping Matt on the shoulder pads.

"I couldn't have done it without Josh's great blocking," Matt said, smiling and taking a gulp of water.

I finally did it! Matt thought. *I finally did it!*

In the second quarter, Matt returned a punt to the Bradley 35-yard line. Jesse threw a great pass to Josh, who caught it and ran the ball to the 4-yard line. Coach sent in the call for a pitchout to Matt to the left side. Matt took the pitchout, and Josh made a beautiful block to open up the left side of the goal line. Matt rushed straight for the corner, full speed, remembering to tuck the ball in close to his body. When the strong Bradley defense shifted and put on a chase, Matt changed direction like a pro, and crossed the goal line without even being touched.

The Alden fans cheered, and after the Panthers scored the extra point, Alden took a commanding 14–0 lead.

Bradley didn't know what to think. Here was the team they thought they could take to the cleaners! They had heard that Alden's running game was their weakest link! And who was that Matt Greene kid? Wasn't this the guy who had fumbled against Lincoln, and thrown the game away?

Woody and the rest of the defense were playing a great game, too. They didn't let Bradley get out of their own territory—they even gave the Bradley punter a good workout.

The Panthers went into the locker room at half-time leading Bradley by the score of 14–0. Coach Wright told them he was proud of them, and to keep doing what they were doing. Coach knew that the Panthers were on fire, and that nobody could stop them now.

"Why don't you let somebody else get a touchdown, Matt?" Josh asked, nudging his friend.

"I bet you'll score one in the second half," Matt said.

And that's exactly what happened.

Bradley came out strong in the second half. They knew that the Panthers were giving most of the calls to Matt, so they concentrated their defense on him. The plan worked for the whole third quarter, and it seemed for a while that Bradley had shut down the Alden offense. At the beginning of the fourth quarter, Bradley scored a touchdown, and then ran the ball in for the two-point conversion, bringing the score to 14–8.

In the last minutes of the fourth quarter, Matt called a time-out and talked to Coach.

"Hey, Coach," Matt said. "I've got an idea. Bradley is expecting me to run. So let's try a delay left, half-back option. I think that will really surprise them."

"Good idea," Coach said. "Go for it."

In the huddle, Matt nudged Josh.

"Hey, Josh," Matt whispered. "I'm going to pass to you. So go long. Go for the bomb."

Josh looked over to his friend with a little smile, and nodded.

Matt got the pitchout, and it was his option whether to run with the ball or pass to Josh. Since no one expected him to pass, the secondary coverage was poor, and Josh was able to get open.

Matt took his arm back and heaved the ball with all his might. He watched the ball fly high up into the air, spinning in a perfect spiral against the blue sky of Cranbrook. The ball landed right in Josh's arms, and he ran it in for the touchdown.

Once again, the Alden fans went nuts. Josh spiked the ball and ran back toward Matt. When the two friends met in the middle of the field, they did their special handshake, fluttering their hands up at the end like birds, and then bursting into laughter.

The final score was Alden 21, Bradley 8. It was only a regular season victory, but the Panthers' locker room was so loud that it seemed like they had just won the championship.

The Panthers would have to wait a while for the *real* championship game. And it turned out to be the most exciting game any one of them had ever seen.

13

During the rest of the season, the Panthers only improved. They worked hard at practice, and played hard in games. When they played Lincoln for the second time, Matt made a special point of scoring big—because Lincoln was the only team to have beaten the Panthers. The final score of the second game against Lincoln was Alden 24, Lincoln 3—and Matt had scored three touchdowns.

Once Matt started playing up to his potential, nobody was able to touch the Panthers. They rolled over every team that came their way, winning one game after the other, and ending the regular season with a record of 8–1. But Bradley ended up with a record of 8–1, too. So at the end of November, it was Bradley versus Alden for the conference championship.

The game was played on a cold Saturday afternoon in Cranbrook. The Panthers had won five straight games, and were confident as they ran out of the locker room. Even though Matt had played five great games in a row, leading the Panthers to victory, all that hard work came down to a single afternoon, *this* afternoon. And he had a feeling this game wouldn't be as easy as the others.

"Let's get 'em," Matt said, slapping Josh on the shoulder pads before the kickoff. "Let's show Bradley who's the boss around here."

"All right!" Josh replied. "Let's get out in front early, and get the momentum on our side."

It didn't work out as Josh had hoped. Matt returned the ball to the 34-yard line—but on the first play of the Panthers' drive, Chuck McPhee fumbled a pass reception, and Bradley ran the ball for a fast touchdown. After only one minute of play, the score was already Bradley 7, Alden 0.

Bradley's early touchdown took the wind out of

the Panthers' sails. Alden's next drive made it almost into Bradley territory, before Jesse threw an incomplete pass, Matt slipped and fell in the backfield for a loss—and the Panthers stalled. Luckily Dan Caner kicked a great punt, which got Alden out of immediate danger.

The Bradley team was on the march. They didn't make amazing plays—no big passes or breakaway runs—but they kept getting first downs, and moving the ball slowly toward the goal line. Woody and the Alden defense were struggling to stop the momentum of the Bradley drive. By the time Bradley had worked its way to the Alden 22-yard line, the Panther defense was getting angry. Standing on the sidelines, Matt could hear the grunts of the defensemen as they crashed into Bradley players, and he could tell that the Panther defense was sick and tired of giving up yardage.

On second and ten from the Panther 22, Dave McShea leapt into the air and swatted down a pass that would have meant another Bradley touchdown. On the next down, the Panther pass coverage was so strong that the Bradley quarterback was forced to throw the ball out of bounds, to avoid getting sacked. At that point, the Bradley field-goal kicker came in, hoping to add three points to the Bradley score. His kick was just right of the goalpost, and Alden escaped without any damage.

At the beginning of the second quarter, the Panther offense seemed to get a little of their momentum back. Matt ran a pitchout from the Panther 37-yard line, dodging and darting all the way to the Bradley 46. It was the first breakaway run of the game, and it pumped up the Panther offense. Matt could feel the new excitement in the huddle.

"Great run, Matt," Jesse said. "Let's keep it going. Thirty-eight, handoff left, with wide receiver blocking, on two. Break!"

Matt crouched down—still breathing hard from his last run, but itching for his next. At the snap, Matt rushed forward and snatched the ball from Jesse's hands. He tucked it tightly in the crook of his arm and cut to the left, where Josh was trying to block a huge Bradley defenseman. Josh slowed the defenseman down long enough for Matt to slip by, leaping over two fallen linemen. Matt saw the safety rushing toward him and turned on his afterburners, sprinting like lightning up the sideline. He was knocked out of bounds at the Bradley 37—just one yard shy of the first down.

The next play was a pass to Chuck McPhee, who was running a post pattern. Chuck had to dive to catch the pass, and he was able to hold onto it for a gain of 15 yards, and a first down.

That was as far as the Panther offense got. With its back against the wall for the first time, the Bradley defense held tight. Matt rushed twice, gaining only two yards on each carry, and then Jesse threw an incomplete pass. Now it was up to the kicker, John DeLuca, to put the Panthers on the board with a field goal.

John kicked soccer style, and had a tendency to pull his kicks to the left. Matt held his breath as he watched the snap and the kick. The ball veered off to the left, and seemed to be heading right for the goalpost. Matt watched in amazement as the ball deflected off the goalpost, and then dropped straight down onto the cross beam. It bounced once on the cross beam before falling over for an Alden field goal!

The crowd went crazy, and everyone mobbed John DeLuca. It was an incredible field goal. And because it was so weird, it gave the Panthers more momentum than a picture-perfect kick would have.

Halfway through the second quarter, the score was Bradley 7, Alden 3. And that was the score when the buzzer rang for halftime.

Heading onto the field for the second half, Matt looked up into the bleachers to find his father. Matt noticed him, waving from the bleachers and standing next to his video camera. Mr. Greene was wearing a huge, proud grin, and giving Matt a big thumbs-up for the second half.

I'm going to score, Matt thought as he waved back. *I can feel it in my bones.*

The Bradley defense didn't agree. For the whole third quarter, the Panthers never even got within field goal range. Jesse's throwing arm was off, and almost all his passes were incomplete. Matt gave each run his best effort, but the Bradley defense was sharper than ever, and kept him from breaking away.

Luckily, the Panther defense was in good form, too, and kept Bradley from putting any points on the board. When the third quarter ended, the score was still Bradley 7, Alden 3.

Matt knew that if Bradley scored again, the game was probably over—and Bradley would be the conference champion. If Alden scored, though, Bradley would still be within easy striking distance. Matt was determined to do something about it.

"We haven't come this far to let Bradley beat us by four lousy points," Matt said to Josh on the sidelines. "All we need is one touchdown to win. Just *one* touchdown."

"Let's get out there and do it!" Josh said, slapping Matt on the helmet.

The Panthers got possession of the ball at their own 35-yard line. The first call was for a pass play, with Josh going long in a sideline flag pattern. Matt hoped that Jesse's arm wouldn't get them into any trouble.

Jesse faded back and waited for Josh to run his pattern. The pass protection was good and Jesse had plenty of time to throw. The ball sailed high into the air, and Josh slowed his pace to try to catch it. He was too late—the defender caught the ball for an interception, and Josh tackled him at the Panther 49-yard line.

"Don't worry about it, Jesse," Matt said, as the Panthers ran off the field. "Shake it off and let's get 'em."

But Matt *was* worried, because Bradley was in excellent position to score and put the game away. And there were only four minutes left in the game.

Bradley played its brand of slow, consistent football, working its way up to the Alden 25. They were also making sure their pass receivers didn't run out of bounds, to keep the clock running. The seconds and minutes kept ticking away—and with them, Alden's hopes for a championship trophy. Soon, the clock read 34 seconds, and Bradley was setting up for a field goal.

Matt held his breath as he watched the kick sail into the air. If the ball went through the uprights, it would as good as clinch the championship. But the kick sailed wide, and the score remained 7–3.

Now there were still only 29 seconds left on the clock.

This is my last chance, Matt thought, as he and the rest of the Alden offense jogged onto the field. He could feel his heart pounding in his chest.

In the huddle, Jesse called the final play. "Pitch to Matt. On two. Come on guys, this is it."

The final seconds seemed to pass in slow motion.

Matt watched the pitch from Jesse float into his arms, and then he turned upfield. Matt could feel his legs pumping. He could hear the grunts of his teammates as they blocked the Bradley defense, and opened up holes in the field.

Matt leapt and dodged his way through the holes, spinning out of tackles and giving head fakes. He looked over to the sideline and saw that he was already at the 50-yard line. A huge bolt of excitement shot through him as he broke the final tackle, and sprinted across 45 yards of empty green turf.

Touchdown!

Matt spiked the ball and ran back into the arms of his teammates. The scoreboard read Alden 9, Bradley 7.

Matt would never forget the feeling of being lifted on top of his teammates' shoulders and being carried off the field, while all the fans went crazy. Even more than that, he would never forget looking up in the bleachers and seeing his father, Big Bill Greene, waving his arms and cheering louder than anyone else.

"Why don't you guys come over to my dad's restaurant?" Matt said to his friends, as they left the locker room that day. "I'm sure he'll give us all a huge celebration feast!"

Big Bill Greene was waiting at the door to his restaurant with a huge smile on his face.

"Here they are!" he cried. "The champions!"

The boys grinned with pride and followed Mr. Greene to a table in the middle of the restaurant.

"You can order anything you want," Mr. Greene said, handing them each a menu. "While you're ordering, why don't you look up at the video screens."

Matt couldn't believe what he saw. It was *him!* Matt saw himself running the ball downfield, to win the championship. He saw himself spinning and twisting and breaking through tackles. His friends clapped and patted Matt on the back as they watched the video.

Then came closeups of Woody, making hard-hitting tackles, and then closeups of Jesse throwing the ball to Josh.

Matt couldn't believe how happy he was. Just then his father set plates of steak and lobster in front of everyone. Matt raised his glass.

"To the Alden Panthers!" he cried.